P9-CLR-693

ESSENTIAL ELEMENTS

A COMPREHENSIVE BAND METHOD

by

Tom C. Rhodes • Donald Bierschenk • Tim Lautzenheiser • John Higgins

Dear Band Student,

Welcome to Essential Elements For Band! We are pleased that you have chosen to play the bassoon. With practice and dedication, you'll enjoy a lifetime of music performance.

Best wishes for your musical success!

Linda Petersen, *Editor*

OF THE BASSOON

The earliest ancestor of the bassoon was called the dulcian. This one piece double reed instrument provided the important bass line in early 16th century music.

Multi-sectioned bassoons first appeared in France in the 17th century. Carl Almenräder (1786-1843) is the most significant contributor to the design of the modern bassoon. He improved the sound and note capabilities of the instrument, and published a paper about his innovations. In 1831, he and A. J. Heckel founded a factory which manufactured the modern German system bassoon.

Originally, there were five members of the bassoon family. The two surviving instruments today are the Bassoon and the Contrabassoon. In concert band and orchestra, these versatile instruments add to the bass line, play solos and blend well with other instruments.

Vivaldi, Mozart, Mahler, Villa-Lobos, Saint-Saëns and Stravinsky are important composers who have included the bassoon in their writing. Famous bassoonists include Bernard Garfield and Sherman Walt.

ISBN 0-7935-1252-2

00863503

Hal Leonard Publishing Corporation
7777 West Bluemound Road P.O. Box 13819 Milwaukee, WI 53213

THE BASICS

Posture

Sit on the edge of your chair, and always keep your:
- Spine straight and tall
- Shoulders back and relaxed
- Feet flat on the floor

Breathing & Air Stream

Breathing is a natural thing we all do constantly. To discover the correct air stream to play your instrument:
- Place the palm of your hand near your mouth.
- Inhale deeply through the corners of your mouth, keeping your shoulders steady. Your waist should expand like a balloon.
- Slowly whisper "tah" as you gradually exhale air into your palm.

The air you feel is the air stream. It produces sound through the instrument. Your tongue is like a faucet or valve in that it releases the air stream.

Producing The Essential Tone

Embouchure (*ahm´-bah-shure*) is your mouth's position on the reed. A good embouchure takes time and effort, so carefully follow these steps for success:
- Soak your reed in a small glass of water.
- Open your mouth so your teeth are slightly apart.
- Pull your jaw back. Keep your jaw in this position when playing bassoon.
- Roll your lower lip over your bottom teeth. Remove the reed from the water glass, and gently put it on the center of your bottom lip.
- Cover your top teeth with your upper lip, and firmly close your lips around the reed. Adjust the reed so your top lip nearly touches the first wire.
- Keep your jaw back. Your lips support the reed. Be sure your teeth do not touch it.

Mouthpiece Work-Outs

Carefully form your embouchure with the reed in place and take a deep breath. Whisper "tah" and gradually exhale your full air stream. Your work-out looks like this:

Getting It Together

Step 1 - Soak your reed (see page 2). Rub a small amount of cork grease on all corks, if needed. Place the seat strap across your chair, or put the neck strap on. Clean hands.

Step 2 - Hold the long joint in your left hand. Grasp the boot joint with your right hand. Gently push the long joint into the larger opening on the boot joint.

Step 3 - Hold the tenor joint in your right hand, and guide it into the remaining opening on the boot joint. Adjust the long joint until the lock is in place.

Step 4 - Place the instrument across your lap. Grasp the bell with your left hand, and press your thumb on the key to lift the connecting lever. Gently twist the bell on the long joint's cork. Align the bridge keys. Insert the hand rest and adjust.

Step 5 - Hold the bocal in your left hand. Gently push the bocal in the small opening of the tenor joint. Align the vent and the whisper key pad. Put the boot joint end of the instrument in the seat strap (or hook the neck strap to the ring) and adjust. Put the reed on the end of the bocal. Hold the bassoon as shown:

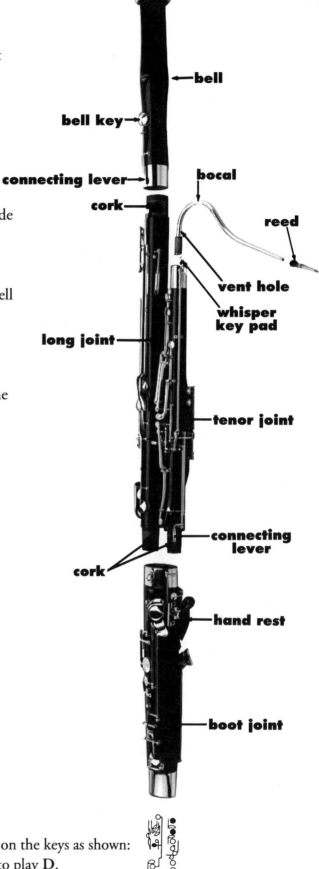

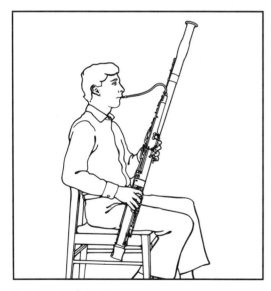

Let's Play!

This special exercise is just for Bassoonists. Place your fingers on the keys as shown: Form the embouchure, take a deep breath and whisper "tah" to play **D**. Try this exercise several times.

Beat • The _Pulse_ of Music

One beat = tap foot **down** on the number and **up** on the "&." Count and tap when playing or resting.

Count **1** & **2** & **3** & **4** &
Tap   ↓ ↑ ↓ ↑ ↓ ↑ ↓ ↑

Fermata ⌒ Hold the note longer, or until your director tells you to release it.

Staff, Bar Lines & Measures

Bar lines divide the music staff into **measures**. The measures on this page have four beats each.

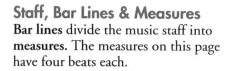

= Music Staff

⌐ Measure ⌐

Bar line

Notes & Rests

Notes tell us how high or low to play _and_ how long to play. Notes are placed on a line or space of the music staff.

Rests tell us to count silent beats.

♩ Quarter Note = 1 Beat
𝄽 Quarter Rest = 1 Silent Beat

1. COUNT AND PLAY

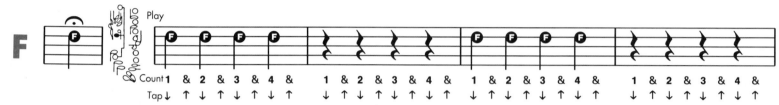

2. A NEW NOTE

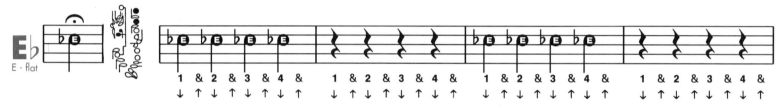

3. TWO'S A TEAM

4. THE NEXT NOTE

5. DOWN AND UP

6. ROLLING ALONG

Go to next line. ▼

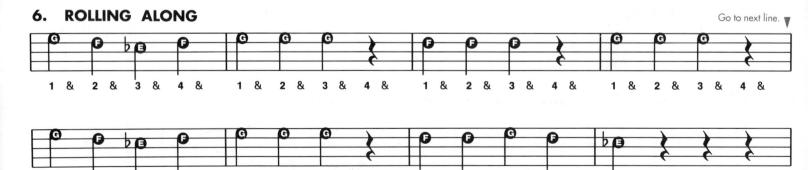

Bass Clef
indicates a new line of music and a set of note names.

Time Signature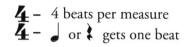
(Meter)
tells us how many beats are in each measure *and* what kind of note gets one beat.

4 – 4 beats per measure
4 – ♩ or 𝄽 gets one beat

Note Names
▲ leger line

Each line and space of the staff has a **note name** that tells us what pitch to play.

Sharp ♯ raises the note and remains in effect for the entire measure. **Flat** ♭ lowers the note and remains in effect for the entire measure. Notes not altered by sharps or flats are called **natural** notes.

NOTE FINGERING REVIEW

Double Bar
indicates the end of a piece of music.

7. LET'S READ MUSIC!

Double bar ▼

▼ Play all E's as E - flats.

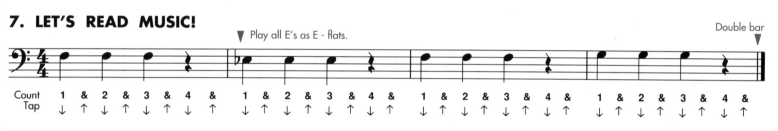

| Count | 1 | & | 2 | & | 3 | & | 4 | & |
| Tap | ↓ | ↑ | ↓ | ↑ | ↓ | ↑ | ↓ | ↑ |

Repeat Sign 𝄇 Go back to the beginning and play the line again.

8. COPY CAT

Repeat from beginning ▼

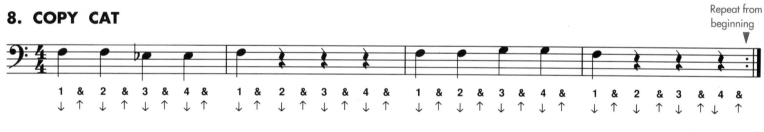

9. ROLLING ALONG

Children's Song

10. FIRST FLIGHT

Repeat ▼

11. ESSENTIAL ELEMENTS QUIZ   Complete the note names before you play.

Note Names   G   E♭   F   G   E♭   E♭ E♭ F G   E♭   E♭

Half Note

♩ = 2 Beats

1 & 2 &
↓ ↑ ↓ ↑

Half Rest

= 2 Silent Beats

1 & 2 &
↓ ↑ ↓ ↑

12. RHYTHM RAP — Count aloud while clapping and tapping.

13. THE HALF COUNTS

14. A NEW NOTE

15. MOVING AROUND

16. ANOTHER NEW NOTE

Breath Mark ' Take a deep breath after you play the note for full value.

17. WALKING

18. MOVING DOWN

B-flat

19. GO TELL AUNT RHODIE

American Folk Song

20. ESSENTIAL ELEMENTS QUIZ — Write in the note names before you play.

Note Names

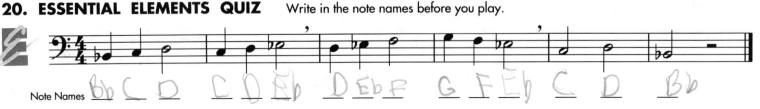

29. EASY STREET

► Correct posture improves your sound. Always sit straight and tall.

30. JUMP ROPE

Theory **Harmony** Two or more different notes played or sung at the same time. A duet is a composition for two players. Practice this duet with a friend, and listen to the harmony.

31. LONDON BRIDGE - Duet   English Folk Song

32. POLLY WOLLY DOODLE

Dynamics *f* *(forte)* Play loudly.   *mf* *(mezzo forte)* Play moderately loud.   *p* *(piano)* Play softly.
Always use full breath support to control your tone at all dynamic levels.

33. CLAP LOUDLY

34. CLAP SOFTLY

35. SKIP TO MY LOU   American Folk Song

36. OLD MACDONALD HAD A BAND

37. ESSENTIAL ELEMENTS QUIZ   Write in the note names to complete this sentence.

O U R B A N D I S T H E G R E A T E S T!

Eighth Notes

2 Eighth Notes = 1 Beat
Play on **down** and **up** taps

A single eighth note has a flag on the stem.

Two eighth notes have a beam across the stem.

38. RHYTHM RAP

39. EIGHTH NOTE TAPS

40. SKIP TO MY LOU IN EIGHTH NOTES

American Folk Song

History Italian composer **Gioachino Rossini** (1792-1868) wrote some of the world's favorite operas. "William Tell" was Rossini's last opera, and its popular theme is still heard on radio and television.

41. WILLIAM TELL

Gioachino Rossini

42. OH, SUSANNA

Stephen Collins Foster

Where is beat 4 ?

43. LONG, LONG AGO

44. ESSENTIAL ELEMENTS QUIZ

Count, clap and tap before you play.

Time Signature **2** – 2 beats per measure
(Meter) **4** – ♩ or 𝄾 gets one beat

Conducting Practice conducting this two-beat pattern.

45. RHYTHM RAP

46. OLD JOE CLARK   Count and clap before you play.
American Folk Song

History One of the world's greatest composers, **Ludwig van Beethoven** (1770-1827), became completely deaf in 1802. Although he could not hear his music like we do, he could "hear" it in his mind. The theme of his last Symphony (No. 9) is called "Ode To Joy." It was composed to the text of a poem by German writer Johann von Schiller. "Ode To Joy" was featured in concerts celebrating the reunification of Germany in 1990.

47. ODE TO JOY
Ludwig van Beethoven

48. HEY, HO! NOBODY'S HOME
Traditional

Dynamics   *crescendo (cresc.)* ◁ Gradually increase volume.
decrescendo (decresc.) ▷ Gradually decrease volume.

49. CLAP THE DYNAMICS

Warm-up Warming up is the proper way to begin a successful performance. After assembling your instrument, carefully set your embouchure. Start your warm-up by playing long tones in the middle register. Then play lower notes, and gradually move into higher notes using easy fingering patterns. Proper breathing and posture are always important.

50. WARM - UP CHORALE #1

51. MICHAEL ROW YOUR BOAT ASHORE - Duet

American Folk Song

Tie A curved line that connects notes of the **same** pitch. Play for the combined counts of the tied notes.

52. FIT TO BE TIED

▼ Hold these tied notes for 2 beats.

53. ALOUETTE

French Folk Song

▼ Hold these tied notes for 3 beats.

Dotted Half Note

♩. = 3 Beats

1 & 2 & 3 &

♩. ◄ Dot
A dot adds half the value of the note.

2 beats + 1 beat = 3 beats

54. RETURN TO ALOUETTE'S PLACE

French Folk Song

American composer **Stephen Collins Foster** (1826-1864) wrote 189 songs, many of which became classic American folk songs. Most of Foster's songs were published shortly before the American Civil War (1860-1865). His works include "Oh, Susanna," "My Old Kentucky Home" and "Camptown Races."

55. CAMPTOWN RACES

Stephen Collins Foster

Tempo The speed of music. Tempo markings are usually written in Italian and are found above the staff.

Andante — Slow walking tempo　　**Moderato** — Moderate tempo　　**Allegro** — Fast bright tempo

56. ESSENTIAL ELEMENTS QUIZ

Moderato

Where is beat 4? ▲

12

Time Signature
(Meter) **3** – 3 beats per measure
4 – ♩ or 𝄽 gets one beat

Conducting Practice conducting this three-beat pattern.

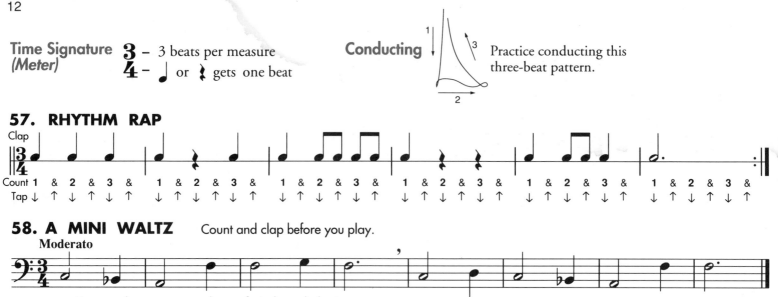

57. RHYTHM RAP

58. A MINI WALTZ   Count and clap before you play.

Moderato

► For your best tone, use plenty of air through the instrument.

History — Norwegian composer **Edvard Grieg** (1843-1907) wrote *Peer Gynt Suite* in 1875 for a play by Henrik Ibsen. Music used in plays, films, radio and television is called **incidental music.** *Peer Gynt Suite* was written the year before the telephone was invented by Alexander Graham Bell. "Morning" is a melody from the first movement of the *Peer Gynt Suite.*

59. MORNING

Edvard Grieg

Accent ♩ or 𝅗𝅥 Emphasize the note.

60. ACCENT YOUR TALENT

History — **Latin American music** combines the folk music from South and Central America, the Caribbean Islands, American Indian, African, Spanish and Portuguese cultures. In this diverse music, melodies feature a lively accompaniment by drums, maracas and claves. Latin American music continues to influence jazz, classical and popular styles of music. This melody, also known as *Chiapanecas,* is a popular children's dance and game song in Latin American countries.

61. MEXICAN CLAPPING SONG

Latin American Folk Song

62. RISING MUFFINS

A♭
A-flat

▲ Remember the ♭ applies to all A's in this measure.

63. ESSENTIAL ELEMENTS QUIZ - RUSSIAN DANCE

1st and 2nd Endings

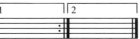

Play the 1st ending the 1st time through. Then, repeat the same section of music, skip the 1st ending and play the 2nd ending.

64. CIRCUS WALTZ

Moderato

mf

1

2 ▼ Hold 4 beats.

2nd time skip to 2nd ending.

65. HATIKVAH

Hebrew Folk Song

Andante

p — *mf* — *p*

History — **Japanese folk music** has origins in ancient China. "Sakura, Sakura" was written for the koto, a 13-string instrument that is over 4000 years old. The unique sound of this ancient Japanese song results from the pentatonic, or five-note sequence used in this tonal system.

66. SAKURA, SAKURA - Full Band Arrangement
(Song of the Blooming Cherry Tree)

Japanese Folk Song
Arr. by John Higgins

Andante

mf — *p*

mf

f > > > > > — *p*

67. THE BIG AIR STREAM

B♭
B - flat

Moderato

mf

▲ Play B♭'s, E♭'s, and all A's as A♭'s in this key signature.

68. JOLLY OLD ST. NICK - Duet

A

f

1

2

B

f

69. TECHNIQUE TRAX

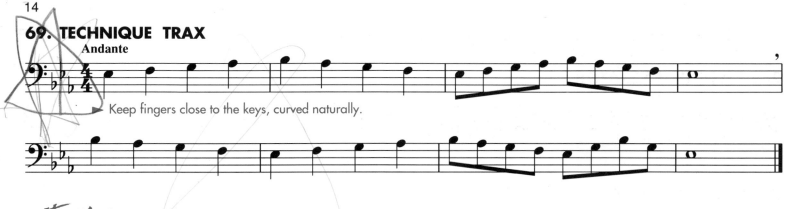

Andante

▶ Keep fingers close to the keys, curved naturally.

Theory — **Theme and Variations** — A musical form where a theme is followed by variations, or different versions, of the theme. A theme is usually a short melody.

70. VARIATIONS ON A FAMILIAR THEME

Theme — *mf* — Variation 1

Variation 2

▲ Play A - naturals.

D.C. al Fine — Play until you see the *D.C. al Fine.* Then, go back to the beginning and play until you see *Fine* (fee'-nay). *D.C.* is the Latin abbreviation for *Da Capo,* or return to the beginning. *Fine* is Latin for "the finish."

71. BANANA BOAT SONG

Latin American Folk Song

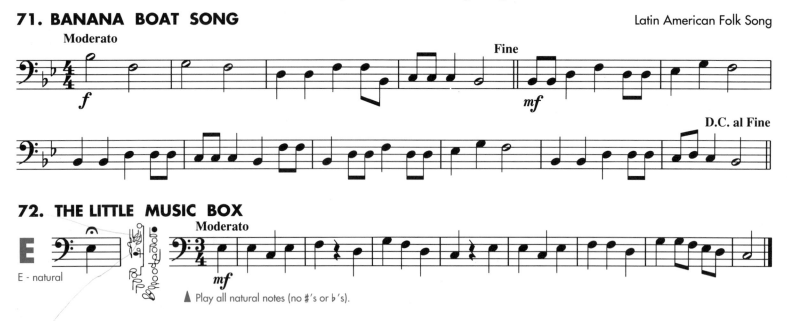

Moderato — *f* — Fine — *mf* — D.C. al Fine

72. THE LITTLE MUSIC BOX

E — E - natural — Moderato — *mf*

▲ Play all natural notes (no #'s or ♭'s).

History — **Black American spirituals** originated in the 1700's. As one of the largest categories of true American folk music, these melodies were sung and passed on for generations without being written down. Black and white people worked together to publish the first spiritual collection in 1867, four years after The Emancipation Proclamation was signed into law. "What A Morning" is a famous Black American spiritual.

73. ESSENTIAL ELEMENTS QUIZ - WHAT A MORNING

Black American Spiritual

Andante — *p* — *mf* — *p* — *mf* — *p* — Fine — D.C. al Fine — *mf* — *p*

Slur  A curved line that connects notes of **different** pitches. Tongue only the first note of each group of notes connected by a slur.

74. SMOOTH OPERATOR

▼ Slur 2 notes. Tongue the first note. Play the next note without tonguing.

75. GLIDING ALONG

Slur 4 notes. Tongue only the first note of notes connected by a slur.

Ragtime is an American music style (1896-1918) that was popular before World War I. It uses early forms of jazz rhythms. Scott Joplin wrote many ragtime piano pieces. The trombones will now learn a *glissando*, a technique used in ragtime and other styles of music.

76. TROMBONE RAG

Phrases Musical sentences that are usually 2 or 4 measures long. Try to play phrases in one breath.

77. THE COLD WIND

A - natural

Multiple Measures Rest The large number tells you how many measures to count and rest. Count each measure in sequence: **1** 2 3 4 | **2** 2 3 4

78. SATIN LATIN

Play Bb's, E - naturals, and A - naturals.

German composer **Johann Sebastian Bach** (1685-1750) wrote hundreds of choral and instrumental works. He was a master teacher, organist and famous improviser. Bach had 21 children, many of whom became famous composers. He wrote this Minuet, or dance in 3/4 time, as a piano teaching piece.

79. ESSENTIAL ELEMENTS QUIZ - MINUET - Duet

Johann Sebastian Bach

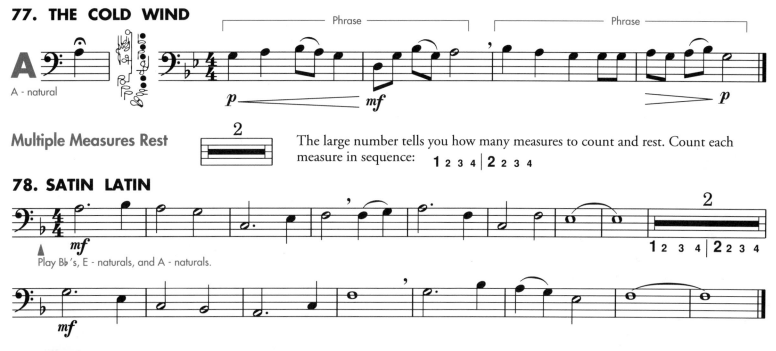

80. WARM - UP CHORALE #2 - FINLANDIA

Jean Sibelius

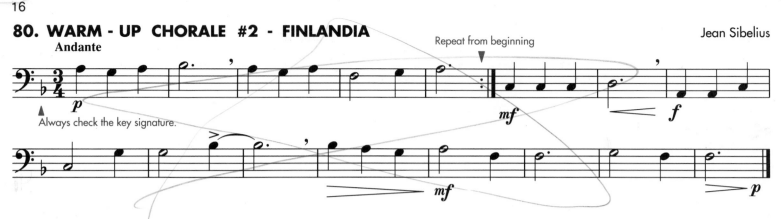

Always check the key signature.

History Austrian composer **Franz Peter Schubert** (1797-1828) was a great composer of songs, symphonies and piano works. He wrote three military marches for piano duet. "March Militaire" is the introduction and theme from one of these popular marches.

Natural Sign ♮ Cancels a flat ♭ or sharp ♯. A natural sign remains in effect for the entire measure.

81. MARCH MILITAIRE

Franz Schubert

82. MY BONNIE LIES OVER THE OCEAN

Scottish Folk Song

The ♭ applies to the tied note. Play the D♭ for 4 beats.

History **Blues** is a form of Black American folk music related to jazz. Boogie-woogie is a blues style first recorded by pianist Clarence "Pine Top" Smith in 1928, one year after Charles Lindbergh's solo flight across the Atlantic. Blues music has altered notes and is usually written in 12 bars, like "Bottom Bass Boogie."

83. BOTTOM BASS BOOGIE - Duet

Great musicians give encouragement to their fellow performers. Clarinetists will now learn a challenging slur pattern, called "Grenadilla Gorilla Jumps." Many clarinets are made of grenadilla wood. Brass players will learn lip slurs, a new warm-up pattern. The success of your band depends on everyone's help and patience. Let's play our best as these sections advance their musical technique.

90. GRENADILLA GORILLA JUMP #1

91. JUMPIN' UP AND DOWN

▲ Play A♮'s.

92. GRENADILLA GORILLA JUMP #2

93. JUMPIN' FOR JOY

Theory · **Interval** The distance between two notes. Starting with "1" on the lower note, count each line and space between the notes. The number of the higher note is the distance of the interval.

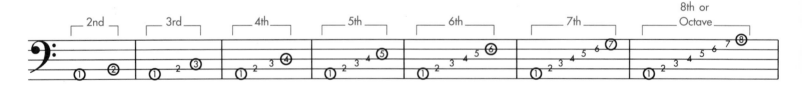

94. GRENADILLA GORILLA JUMP #3

95. JUMPIN' JACKS

96. ESSENTIAL ELEMENTS QUIZ   Write in the numbers of the intervals. Remember to count **up** from the lowest note.

Interval Numbers ___2nd___ _____ _____ _____ _____ _____ _____

97. GRENADILLA GORILLA JUMP #4

98. THREE IS THE COUNT

Draw in the bar lines before you play.

99. DIXIE

Dan Emmett

▲ Play Bb's, Eb's, and Ab's.

100. GRENADILLA GORILLA JUMP #5

101. TECHNIQUE TRAX

Theory **Trio** A composition for three players. Practice this trio with two other players and listen for 3-part harmony.

102. KUM BAH YAH - Trio

African Spiritual

A Moderato

B Moderato

Bass Line Moderato

103. AUSTRIAN WALTZ

Austrian Folk Song

mf

104. BOTANY BAY

Australian Folk Song

Moderato

mf

f

mf

Time Signature (Meter) **C** Common Time
Same as 4/4

Conducting Practice conducting this four-beat pattern.

105. TECHNIQUE TRAX

► Keep your fingers close to the keys, curved naturally.

Theory **Rounds or Canons** A musical form where performers play or sing the same melody and enter at different times. This is called **counterpoint**, a type of harmony. Divide into groups, and play "Kookaburra" as a 2-part round.

106. KOOKABURRA - Round

Australian Folk Song

1   2

107. UP ON THE HOUSETOP - Duet

Allegro

B.R. Hanby

A

f

B   Allegro

f

Theory **Meter Change** Occasionally, the meter (time signature) changes in music. Watch for meter changes and count carefully.

108. ESSENTIAL ELEMENTS QUIZ - METER MANIA #1 Count and clap before playing. Can you conduct this?

mf

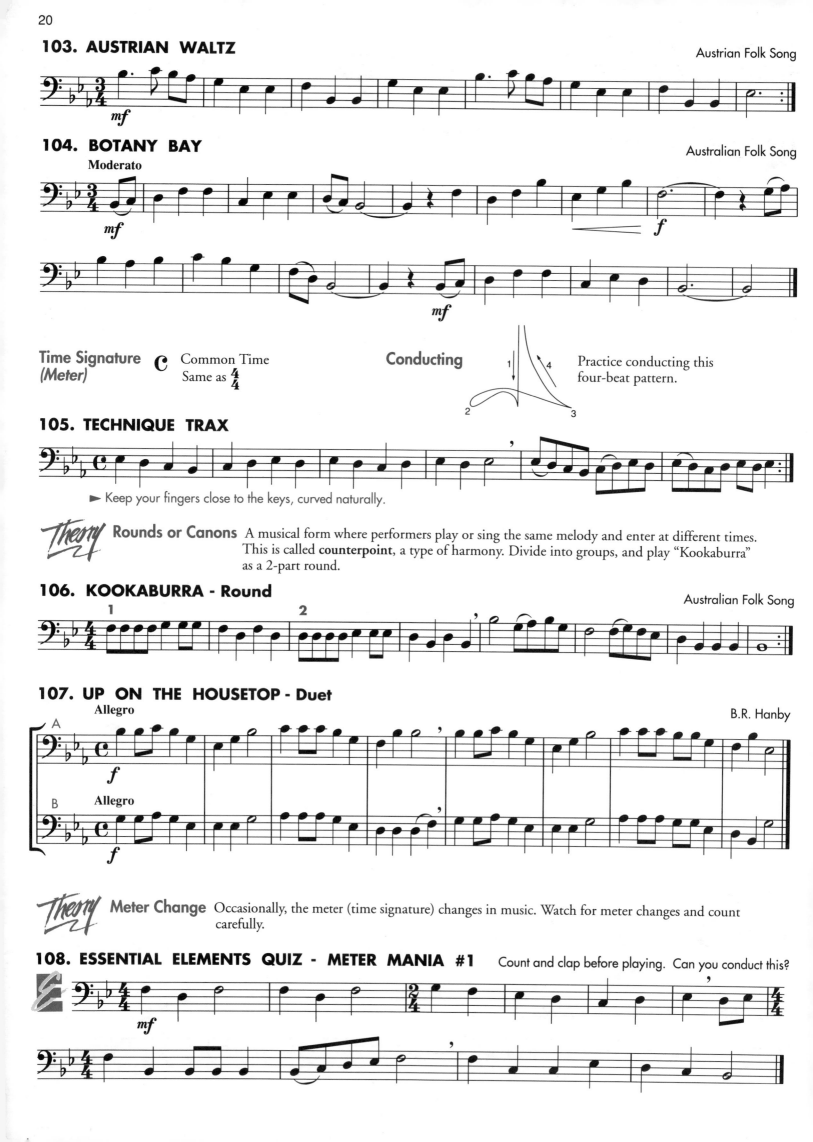

109. EASY JUMPS

110. TECHNIQUE TRAX

Moderato

▲ Always check the key signature.

111. GERMAN FOLK SONG

Moderato

Repeat Sign 𝄆 𝄇 Repeat the section of music enclosed by the repeat signs 𝄆 𝄇

112. WHEN THE SAINTS GO MARCHIN' IN

American Folk Song

Allegro

113. LOWLAND GORILLA WALK

114. SMOOTH SAILING

115. MORE EASY JUMPS

▲ Play A♮'s.

116. CAREFUL CLARINET COVER

117. SCHOOL SPIRIT - Full Band Arrangement

W. T. Purdy
Arr. by John Higgins

March Style

History

Austrian composer **Franz Josef Haydn** (1732-1809) wrote 104 symphonies. Many of these works had nicknames, including "The Surprise" Symphony No. 94. In the soft second movement, Haydn deliberately added sudden loud dynamics to wake up an often-sleepy audience. Here is that famous theme. Pay special attention to the dynamics.

118. SURPRISE SYMPHONY THEME

Franz Josef Haydn

119. YOU ARE A PERCUSSIONIST

Hand Claps

Foot Stomps

120. ESSENTIAL ELEMENTS QUIZ - THE STREETS OF LAREDO

American Folk Song

Write in the note names before you play.

Note Names ____ ____ ____ ____ ____ ____ ____ ____

Theory **Scale** A sequence of notes in ascending or descending order. The first and last notes of most scales are the same as the name of the scale. The interval between these two notes is called an **octave**.

121. CONCERT Bb SCALE (Your Bb Scale) Memorize this exercise.

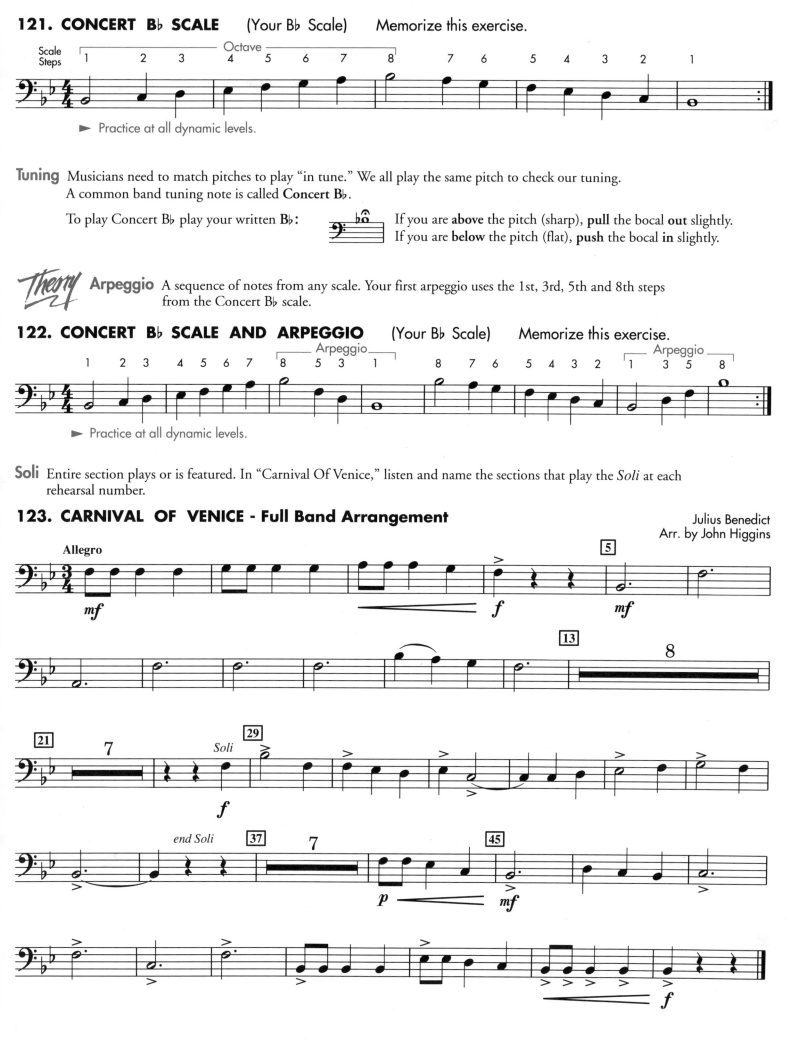

► Practice at all dynamic levels.

Tuning Musicians need to match pitches to play "in tune." We all play the same pitch to check our tuning. A common band tuning note is called **Concert Bb**.

To play Concert Bb play your written Bb: If you are **above** the pitch (sharp), **pull** the bocal **out** slightly.
If you are **below** the pitch (flat), **push** the bocal **in** slightly.

Theory **Arpeggio** A sequence of notes from any scale. Your first arpeggio uses the 1st, 3rd, 5th and 8th steps from the Concert Bb scale.

122. CONCERT Bb SCALE AND ARPEGGIO (Your Bb Scale) Memorize this exercise.

► Practice at all dynamic levels.

Soli Entire section plays or is featured. In "Carnival Of Venice," listen and name the sections that play the *Soli* at each rehearsal number.

123. CARNIVAL OF VENICE - Full Band Arrangement

Julius Benedict
Arr. by John Higgins

124. A DANCING MELODY

Moderato

History American composer and conductor **John Philip Sousa** (1854-1932) wrote 136 marches. Known as "The March King," Sousa wrote *The Stars And Stripes Forever, Semper Fidelis, The Washington Post* and many other patriotic pieces. Sousa's band performed all over the country, and his fame helped boost the popularity of bands in America. Here is a melody from his famous *El Capitan* operetta and march.

125. EL CAPITAN

John Philip Sousa

Allegro

Play A♮'s.

History "O Canada," formerly known as "National Song," was first performed in French Canada during 1880. Robert Stanley Weir translated the English version in 1908. It was officially adopted as the national anthem of Canada in 1980, one hundred years after its premier.

126. O CANADA

Calixa Lavallee,
l'Hon. Judge Routhier
and Justice R.S. Weir

Maestoso (Majestically)

127. ESSENTIAL ELEMENTS QUIZ - METER MANIA #2

Count and clap before playing. Can you conduct this?

Theory **Enharmonics** Notes that are written differently but sound the same and are played with the same fingerings. Your fingering chart (pgs. 30-31) shows the enharmonic notes and fingerings for your instrument..

128. SNAKE CHARMER

G♭/F♯

G - flat   F - sharp

mf

Enharmonic notes. Use the same fingering.

129. CLOSE ENCOUNTERS

D♭/C♯

D - flat   C - sharp

mf

Enharmonic notes. Use the same fingering.

130. NOTES IN DISGUISE

mf   *p*   *mf*

Theory **Chromatics** Notes that are altered with sharps, flats and naturals. The smallest distance between two notes is called a **half-step**. A scale made up of consecutive half-steps is called a **chromatic scale**.

131. HALF - STEPPIN'

mf

History French composer **Camille Saint-Saëns** (1835-1921) wrote many operas, suites, symphonies and chamber works. His famous opera *Samson et Delila* was written in 1877, the same year that Thomas Edison invented the phonograph. "Egyptian Dance" is one of the main opera themes from *Samson et Delila*.

132. EGYPTIAN DANCE

Camille Saint- Saëns

mf

Russian composer **Peter Illyich Tchaikovsky** (1840-1893) wrote 6 symphonies, 3 ballets and hundreds of other works. He was a master at writing popular melodies. His *1812 Overture* and this famous melody from *Capriccio Italien* were both written in 1880, one year after Thomas Edison invented an improved light bulb.

133. CAPRICCIO ITALIEN

Peter I. Tchaikovsky

▲ Play A♮'s.

134. AMERICAN PATROL

F.W. Meacham

135. WAYFARING STRANGER

Black American Spiritual

136. ESSENTIAL ELEMENTS QUIZ - CONCERT B♭ SCALE COUNTING CONQUEST

Performing for an audience is an exciting part of being involved in music. This solo is based on Johannes Brahms' **Symphony No. 1 in C Minor, Op. 68.** Brahms was a German composer who lived from 1833-1897. He completed his first symphony in 1876, the same year that Alexander Graham Bell invented the telephone. You and a piano accompanist can perform for the band, your school and at other occasions.

137. THEME FROM SYMPHONY NO. 1 - Solo (E♭ Concert version)

Johannes Brahms
Arr. by John Higgins

138. AMERICA THE BEAUTIFUL - Full Band Arrangement

Samuel A. Ward
Arr. by John Higgins

139. LA CUCARACHA - Full Band Arrangement

Latin American Folk Song
Arr. by John Higgins

140. THEME FROM 1812 OVERTURE - Full Band Arrangement

Peter I. Tchaikovsky
Arr. by John Higgins

Allegro

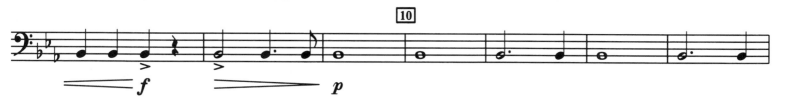

BASSOON FINGERING CHART

Take Special Care

Before putting your instrument back in its case after playing, do the following:

• Carefully remove the reed and blow air through it. Return to reed case.

• Remove the bocal and blow air through one end to remove excess moisture.

• Take the instrument apart in the reverse order of assembly. Swab out each section with a cloth swab or cleaning rod. Drop the weight of the swab through each section and pull it through. Return each section to the correct spot in the case.

◯ = OPEN

● = PRESSED DOWN

◒ = HALF HOLE COVERED

The most common fingering appears first when two fingerings are shown.

Instrument courtesy of
Yamaha Corporation of America
Band and Orchestral Division.

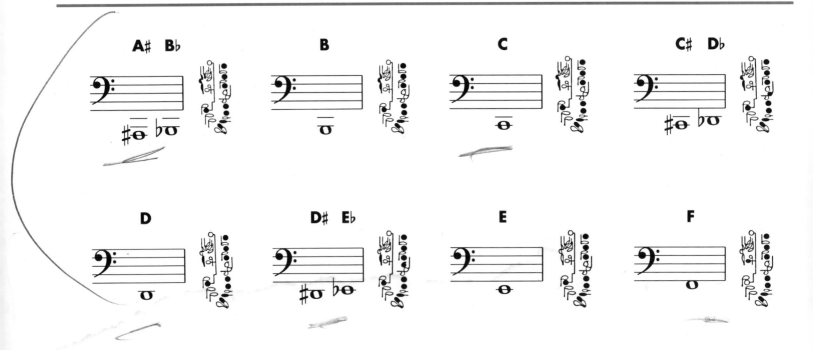

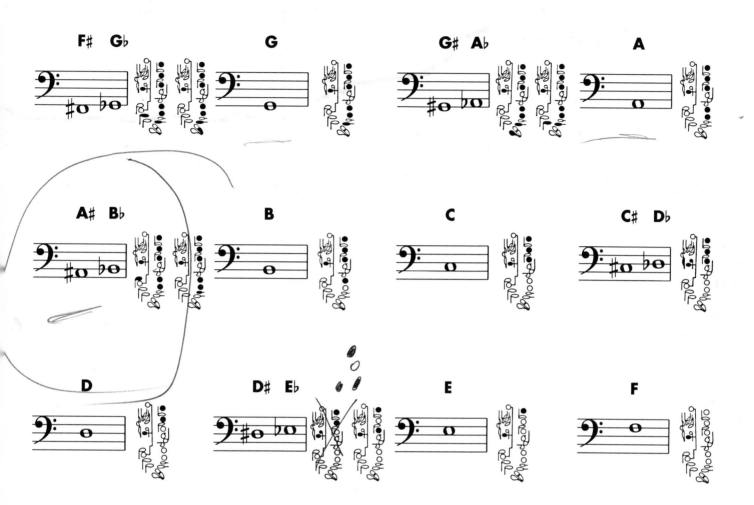

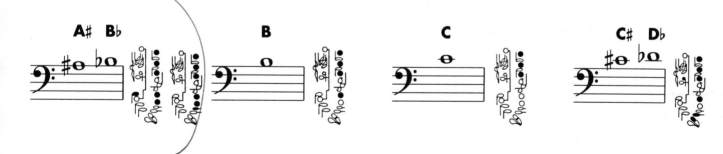

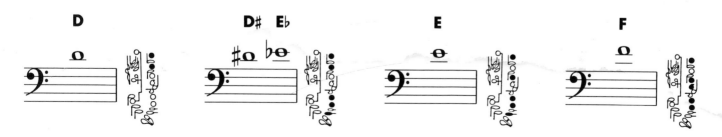

GLOSSARY

Essential Element	Definition	Essential Element	Definition
Accent	Emphasize the note.	Lip Slurs	Brass instrument exercise of playing slurred notes without changing valves.
Allegro	Fast bright tempo.	Measure	A segment of music divided by bar lines.
Andante	Slow walking tempo.		
Arpeggio	A sequence of notes from any scale.	Meter Change	A meter (time signature) change in music.
Bach, Johann Sebastian	German composer (1685-1750).		
Bar Lines	Divide the music staff into measures.	*mezzo forte* *mf*	Play moderately loud.
Bass Clef	"F" clef used by trbs., bar, bsn. and tuba.	Moderato	Moderate tempo.
Beat	The pulse of music.	Mozart, Wolfgang Amadeus	Austrian composer (1756-1791).
Beethoven, Ludwig van	German composer (1770-1827).	Multiple Measures Rest	The number indicates how many measures to count and rest.
Black American Spirituals	Music style originating in the 1700's.		
Blues	Music form and style related to jazz.	Music Staff	Lines and spaces where notes are placed.
Breath Mark	Take a deep breath after playing the note full value.	Natural Sign ♮	Cancels a flat ♭ or sharp ♯ in the measure.
Chromatics	Notes that are altered with sharps, flats and naturals.	Notes	Tell us how high or low to play *and* how long to play.
Chromatic Scale	Sequence of notes in half-steps.	Phrases	Musical sentences that are usually 2 or 4 measures long.
Common Time ℂ	Another way to write 4/4.		
Concert B♭	Band tuning note.	*piano* *p*	Play softly.
Crescendo	Gradually increase volume.	Pick-up Notes	Note or notes that come before the first full measure.
D.C. al Fine	*Da Capo al Fine* - Play until *D.C. al Fine.* Go back to the beginning and play until *Fine.*	Rehearsal Numbers	Measure numbers in squares above the staff.
Decrescendo	Gradually decrease volume.	Repeat Sign	Go back to the beginning and play again.
Dotted Note	The dot adds half the value of the note.		Repeat the section of music enclosed by repeat signs.
Double Bar	Indicates the end of a piece of music.	Ragtime	Music style popular from 1896-1918.
Duet	Composition for two players.	Rests	Silent beats of music.
Dvořák, Antonin	Bohemian composer (1841-1904).	Rossini, Gioachino	Italian composer (1792-1868).
Dynamics	The volume of music.	Round or Canon	Musical form where instruments play the same melody entering at different times.
Embouchure	Position of your mouth on the mouthpiece.		
Enharmonics	Notes that are written differently but sound the same.	Saint-Saëns, Camille	French composer (1835-1921).
Fermata ⌢	Hold the note longer, or until your director tells you to release it.	Scale	Sequence of notes in ascending or descending order.
1st and 2nd Endings	Play the 1st ending the 1st time through. Then, repeat the same music skip the 1st ending and play the 2nd.	Schubert, Franz Peter	Austrian composer (1797-1828).
		Sharp ♯	Raises the note and remains in effect the entire measure.
Flat ♭	Lowers the note and remains in effect the entire measure.	Slur	A curved line that connects notes of different pitches.
forte *f*	Play loudly.	Soli	Entire section plays or is featured.
Foster, Stephen Collins	American composer (1826-1864).	Sousa, John Philip	American composer (1854-1932).
Glissando *gliss.*	Slide from one note to another.	Tchaikovsky, Peter Illyich	Russian composer (1840-1893).
Grieg, Edvard	Norwegian composer (1843-1907).	Tempo	The speed of music.
Half-step	The smallest distance between two notes.	Theme and Variations	Musical form where a theme is followed by variations of the theme.
Harmony	Two or more different notes played or sung at the same time.	Tie	A curved line that connects notes of the same pitch.
Haydn, Franz Josef	Austrian composer (1732-1809).	Time Signature (Meter)	Tells how many beats are in each measure and what kind of note gets one beat.
Interval	The numerical distance between two notes.		
Japanese Folk Music	Music from Japan.	Treble Clef	"G" clef used by fls., ob., clar., sax. and tpt.
Key Signature	Flats or sharps next to the clef that apply to entire piece.	Trio	Composition for three players.
Latin American Music	Music from Latin American cultures.	Tuning	Matching pitches, listening and instrument adjusting.
Leger Lines	Adds notes outside of the music staff.		